Saints for Boys

NIHIL OBSTAT: John A, Goodwine, J.C.D.
                  Censor Librorum

IMPRIMATUR: ✠ Francis Cardinal Spellman
                  Archbishop of New York
                  April 11, 1961

ISBN: 978-1-939094-20-9

Printed and bound in the United States of America.

Neumann Press
Charlotte, North Carolina
www.NeumannPress.com
2014

Saints for Boys

BY ALMA SAVAGE

PICTURES BY
WILLIAM DE J. RUTHERFOORD

NEUMANN PRESS
Charlotte, North Carolina

Contents

SAINT ALOYSIUS GONZAGA

Little Aloysius Gonzaga lived in a castle in Italy. His father was a great soldier.

Aloysius liked to watch his father's men marching. He liked to march with them, too.

Once, when no one was looking, he loaded a cannon and fired it. There was a great "Bang!" Everyone in camp was frightened, for they thought an enemy had come.

When Aloysius was eleven years old, he read about priests who went to faraway places as missionaries. "Maybe I will become a priest instead of a soldier," Aloysius thought.

He was too young to go to far-off lands to teach people about God. But he thought, "I will teach people right here at home." Soon he began to give catechism lessons to the poor boys who lived nearby.

This made him happy, but it ended when he became a page at the court of a prince. Aloysius did not like being a page, but he offered his work to God. "This is what God wants me to do, and I will do it well," he said.

Even at court, Aloysius dreamed of being a priest. One day he told his father about his dream. The father shouted, "You will be a soldier! Put this nonsense out of your mind."

Aloysius prayed hard, and at last his father said, "Very well! Become a priest if that is what you want."

At once Aloysius went to Rome to study. He studied hard and prayed hard. He helped in the kitchen and with the cleaning, too. And everything he did, he did as well as he could, for the love of God.

Saint Aloysius Gonzaga is now the patron saint of boys. As a child, he had loved God and always tried to obey Him. Now every boy can pray to Saint Aloysius and try to do God's will as he did.

SAINT VINCENT DE PAUL

Vincent de Paul was a poor boy who lived on a tiny farm in France. He and his five brothers and sisters helped their father on the farm.

Vincent's part of the work was to take the sheep to pasture. But on rainy days the pasture was very muddy. Then Vincent made stilts so that he could walk through the mud.

When Vincent grew up, he became a priest in a poor country parish. One day he told his people about a family that lived nearby. "Everyone in that family is sick," said Father Vincent. "They are so poor that they have no food, and there is no one to take care of them."

That afternoon he saw the people of his parish going to visit the sick family. Each one was carrying some food.

Vincent said to his people, "You are taking care of that family today. But who will take care of them tomorrow? Let us take turns helping our poor neighbors. Then they will always have food and care."

And that is just what the people did.

Soon after, Father Vincent went to live in the city. Some people there were rich, but Vincent saw many who were very poor. Some were sick and no one helped them. Others never had enough to eat. Many little children had no place to live.

Vincent asked the rich people to give him money, and with it he built homes for poor children and hospitals for the sick. He gave food to poor people. He was the friend of anyone who needed help.

Then some rich ladies said, "Father, you cannot do all the work yourself. Let us help you to care for the poor." These good ladies became the first Sisters of Charity, and they did Vincent's work well.

Saint Vincent was kind to everyone. Let us pray that we may be that way, too.

SAINT DOMINIC SAVIO

Dominic Savio lived in a village in Italy. When he was five years old, he became an altar boy. He was happy to serve at Mass, for he liked to be near our Lord.

A few years later, Dominic started to go to a school two miles away. To get there he had to walk along a country road.

One day a man said, "Dominic, aren't you afraid to walk this road alone?"

"Oh, I am never alone," Dominic answered. "My Guardian Angel is always with me."

One day at school, the teacher blamed Dominic for something he had not done. "You should be punished," the teacher said to him. "Stand up so that your friends may see the boy who has been so bad."

The other boys looked at Dominic, but he did not say one word.

The next day the teacher called to Dominic and said, "I am sorry, Dominic. I have just heard that it was another boy who did that bad thing. Why didn't you tell me?"

Dominic said, "I thought of our Lord. People accused Him of things He hadn't done. And Jesus did not say one word to help Himself."

When Dominic was twelve years old, he went to the school of Don Bosco, a holy priest. Dominic and Don Bosco soon became good friends. The boys in school liked Dominic, too, for he was always ready to help them.

One day Dominic heard that two angry boys were going to have a fight. He saw that each boy had a pile of stones to throw. "Come on. Be friends," said Dominic. But the boys would not listen.

At once Dominic stepped between them. "Go away," the boys said to him. "Our stones will hit you, and we don't want that."

Then Dominic took out his crucifix and held it up. He said, "If you won't throw stones at me, throw them at our Lord." The boys were ashamed and they shook hands.

After a few years Dominic died. Don Bosco was not sad, for he knew that his young friend was with Jesus and Mary.

We can pray to Saint Dominic Savio and ask him to help us to do everything for God's glory, just as he did.

Saint Francis

Long ago in the town of Assisi in Italy,
   there lived a boy named Francis.
His father sold cloth,
   and he was very rich.

Francis grew up to be
a lively young man.
He liked parties and fun.
He played music and sang,
and he had many friends.

One day Francis ran off
    to join the army.
He was wounded and put in prison.
After a long while,
    the enemy set him free.

When he got home, he was thin and tired.
He was no longer full of fun.
Now he knew what it was like
to be alone and sick and poor.

One day Francis went into an old,
    broken-down church.
As he prayed, he heard a voice say,
    "My house is falling apart.
    Repair it, my son."
Francis knew that God
    had spoken to him.

ONCE, while SAINT FRANCIS was praying, Jesus told him, "I want you to show people how to love Me. You can do this by becoming poor, as I was." Being like Jesus filled Francis with joy. People asked him, "How can we have your joy?"

Dear God, help me to know the joy of giving
because of love for You.

Francis said, "It is easy to be full of God's joy when you stop loving so many things here on earth. God is all I want or need." People followed Francis; they knew he walked in the footsteps of Jesus.

Francis loved everything that God made. He praised God for the sun; he loved birds and animals. "But most of all," he said, "I love people. Jesus came to put His own life into people."

Dear Jesus, help me to love people;
You died on the Cross to make them worth loving.

More and more Francis helped the poor.
One day he gave away money and cloth
   that belonged to his father.
"You must not give away things
   that are not yours," said his father.

Francis was sorry for what he had done.
He took off his fine clothes,
   and put on the clothes of a poor man.

Now Francis was as poor as any beggar.
He grew to love God so very much
    that he decided to live for God alone.
Other people followed him,
    and they called themselves Franciscans.

Francis loved everything that God made.
Once he tamed a wolf
   that was fierce and wild.
The wolf was very hungry,
   and it went into a town to look for food.

The people were afraid of the wolf.
It ate their sheep,
    and it even ran after the children.

Francis spoke to it and said,
  "You must stop, Brother Wolf.
  Be good, and the people
  will always give you food."
The wolf was ashamed.
And never again did it hurt anyone
  in that town.

Francis loved the birds, too.
They listened when he talked to them,
and he spoke to them about God.

Francis died
    singing praises to God.
His body showed
    the same wounds
    that our Lord
    bore on the cross.
The wounds were signs
    of God's love
    for this holy man,
    Saint Francis.
The feast of Saint Francis
    is on October 4.

The Archangel Gabriel

THE ANGEL GABRIEL carried messages from God to men. One day he came to Mary saying, "Hail, full of grace! The Lord is with thee."

Our Blessed Lady could not understand these
words. Then the Angel Gabriel said, "God
wants you to become the Mother of Jesus."
Mary answered, "God's will be done."

*Dear God, help me to listen when my Guardian Angel
tells me what to do.*

45

Saint Joseph

Good saint joseph became the foster-father of Jesus. The Angel Gabriel came to Joseph and said, "Take Mary as your wife. She needs you to guard her and protect the Baby Jesus."

Then Joseph and Mary left Nazareth. He had a hard time finding a place in Bethlehem where Jesus could be born.

Dear Saint Joseph, tell Jesus that I love Him.
Help me to be good like you.

The wicked King Herod wanted to kill Jesus.
Again God's Angel came to Joseph saying,
"Take Jesus and His Mother to Egypt." It was
a long journey.

Joseph looked after Jesus and Mary. Later he took them back to his home in Nazareth. Joseph was a carpenter. He liked to help people build happy homes.

Dear Saint Joseph, help me to make our home a happy one.

Saint Joseph still looks after the things that belong to Jesus. Here on earth Jesus loves His Church most. Saint Joseph protects the Church all over the world. We belong to Jesus when we belong to His Church.

Saint Patrick

Saint patrick was kidnapped by pirates when he was a boy. They carried him off to Ireland. He saw the people there dance around false gods.

Patrick felt sorry. He said, "With God's help I'll escape and come back to teach them about the true God."

Dear God, I thank You for letting me know about You.

Patrick kept asking God to help him. He became a priest, and later a bishop. Then the Pope sent him to Ireland. One day he showed a shamrock to the people. "See this stem with three leaves," he said. "Let it remind you that in the one true God there are three divine Persons."

I adore You, dear God, Father, Son, and Holy Ghost.

Saint Benedict

WHEN SAINT BENEDICT was a boy he looked up and said, "See how the sun and stars obey God. They are never late. They never run into each other. They work in good order. If people would obey God they would get along better with each other and everybody would be much happier."

Benedict spent his whole life loving God and showing people how to be happy by doing what God wants. Benedict wrote down rules to help people live happily. Here are some of them:

1. Keep busy, and you will not have time to listen to the devil.

Dear God, help me to work and pray and to obey out of love for You.

2. Offer all your work and play as a prayer.

3. Remember that you obey God when you listen to your father and mother.

Saint Dominic

Saint dominic began to love God when he was a boy. Sometimes he preached little sermons to tell his playmates how he felt about God.

Dominic said, "We must help people to get to heaven. We must love each other as Jesus loves us. People are very dear to God, and they must be dear to us too."

Dear Jesus, help me to love You, and to teach others to love You too.

The Blessed Mother of Jesus helped Dominic do his work. She told him to teach the Rosary to everyone.

Dear Jesus, when I pray the Rosary, help me to think of all the ways You showed Your love for me.

Saint Michael, the Archangel

G<small>OD</small> made S<small>AINT</small> M<small>ICHAEL</small> and all the angels before He made men. God told the angels to love and serve Him. Many proud ones said, "No, we will not." Then they became devils and Michael drove them into hell.

Saint Michael is still fighting on God's side. After Mass we ask Saint Michael to help us fight the devil. We also pray that bad people become good again.

Dear God, help me to fight against everything bad.

Before We Begin to Pray

R<small>EMEMBER</small> that God is close to us, looking at us and listening to us. Remember that He loves us, and wants us to talk to Him.

The Sign of the Cross

*In the Name of the Father, and of the Son,
and of the Holy Ghost, Amen.*

In the Name of the Father

and of the Son   *and of the Holy Ghost*   *Amen.*

THE SIGN of the cross is the most beautiful of all
signs. It means that there is One God, who is
great and good and beautiful, and that He is Three
Persons. The First Person is God the Father, who
made us out of nothing. The Second Person is God
the Son, who came from heaven to save us. His
name is Jesus. He comes to live in us in Holy Communion. The Third Person is God the Holy Ghost.
He is all love and goodness. He makes things live
and grow, and He helps us to be holy.

The sign of the cross reminds us that Jesus, the Son of God, died on a cross. He died in such a hard way because He loves us and wants us to love Him.

We should make the sign of the cross carefully and with love. Then good and holy thoughts fill our hearts.

We make the sign of the cross when we wake up, and before we go to sleep. We make it when we go into church, and before and after we pray, and before we eat or drink. We often make it before we go somewhere, or when we begin to work or play. Then we do these things in God's Name, to please Him, and God blesses us.

The Our Father

Our Father, who art in Heaven, hallowed be Thy Name. Thy Kingdom come, Thy Will be done on earth, as it is in heaven. Give us this day our daily bread, and forgive us our trespasses, as we forgive those who trespass against us. And lead us not into temptation, but deliver us from evil. Amen.

WHEN JESUS, God's Son, came down from heaven to be with us, He had many things to teach us. He wanted to tell us about God, His Father. He wanted to tell us about what heaven is like, and what we should do to go there. The people had seen Him pray to God, His Father, every day, and sometimes all night. One day someone asked Him, "Lord, teach us how to pray." And so Jesus taught them the Our Father.

The Our Father is the best of all prayers. When we say it, Jesus prays with us. That makes our prayers very strong and holy, because Jesus is God. We pray with Jesus, and with all the Christian people in the world. Our prayers go up to God all together, like one big voice.

The Our Father teaches us that we should not spend all our time asking God for things. We should start out by loving and praising God, and we should pray for God's Kingdom—for God to be known and loved everywhere. We should forgive other people who have been mean to us, if we want God to forgive us our sins. And we should ask God to help us be good.

The Hail Mary

Hail Mary, full of grace! The Lord is with thee; blessed art thou among women, and blessed is the fruit of thy womb, Jesus. Holy Mary, Mother of God, pray for us sinners, now and at the hour of our death. Amen.

WE CANNOT look straight at the sun. It is too bright and beautiful. God is bright and beautiful too, and we cannot see Him with our eyes. His brightness is called "grace."

When God made the first man and woman, Adam and Eve, their souls were bright with grace. But Adam and Eve did not stay good. They sinned and lost God's grace. After that, nobody in the world had any grace. Nobody was fit to be God's friend. Heaven's door was shut. A dead bird or a dead kitten is not like a live one. Life is gone. Grace is God's life. People's souls are dead when they have no grace.

God wanted to give us grace again. He started by making a new little girl with grace in her soul. The little girl's name was Mary. When Mary grew up to be a young lady, God sent one of His great angels to visit her.

The angel bowed low, and said, "Hail, Mary, full of grace! The Lord is with thee!"

The angel told Mary a secret. He told her she was going to have a baby, and the baby would be God's Son!

Mary said, "I will do whatever God wants."

After a while Mary's baby was born. His name was Jesus. Jesus is God's Son, and He has God's brightness and beauty. That is what we mean when we say, "Blessed is the fruit of thy womb, Jesus." That is what Mary's cousin, Elizabeth, said when Mary came to visit her.

When Jesus grew up, He died on the cross and opened heaven for us. He brought back grace for everybody in the whole world. Mary stood by the cross and cried when Jesus died. We want Mary to pray for us now and when we die, too. We say, "Holy Mary, Mother of God, pray for us sinners, now and at the hour of our death. Amen."

Morning Prayer to the Guardian Angel

Angel of God, my guardian dear,
To whom His love commits me here;
Ever this day be at my side,
To light and guard, to rule and guide
    Amen.

WHEN we are born, God gives each one of us a brave, bright angel to watch over us and take care of us. The angel is our guardian. He stays with us while we grow. All through life, the angel is at our side. When we die, the angel takes our soul to God.

Night Prayer to the Guardian Angel

Angel of God, my guardian dear,
To whom His love commits me here;
Ever this night be at my side,
To light and guard, to rule and guide.
Amen.

THE ANGELS always see God's beautiful face,
even when they are busy here taking care of us.
We cannot see our angel, but we can talk to him.
He likes us to remember he is always there. He
likes to do special things for us, and he will do
many nice things if we ask him. We ought to be
good friends with our angel.

72

Glory be to the Father, and to the Son, and to the Holy Ghost. As it was in the beginning, is now, and ever shall be, world without end. Amen.

God never had a beginning. He always was. But God was not alone, for He is One God in Three Persons. We call Him the Blessed Trinity. Blessed Trinity means three Persons in One God.

When we pray "Glory be to the Father," we are praying to God, the Blessed Trinity. We are saying the best kind of prayer—one which does not ask for something. It is praising God. It means, "God the Father, and God the Son, and God the Holy Ghost, you are wonderful and holy. You were always wonderful and holy, and you always will be. I cannot understand you, but I love you forever and ever. I want everybody in the world to love and praise you."

Morning Offering

My God, I offer Thee this day
All that I think or do or say,
Uniting it to what was done
On earth by Jesus Christ, Thy Son.

WE DO not have to talk to God all the time. We can please God by thinking about Him and by doing our work and play for Him.

It is nice to say the morning offering when we wake up. That gives God everything we do that day, together with what Jesus did when He lived in our world. We must make up our minds, of course, to do and think and say only nice things, the kind Jesus would do. He did kind and loving things all day long.

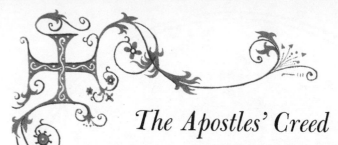

The Apostles' Creed

I believe in God, the Father Almighty, Creator of Heaven and earth; and in Jesus Christ, His only Son, Our Lord; who was conceived by the Holy Ghost, born of the Virgin Mary, suffered under the Pontius Pilate, was crucified, died, and was buried. He descended into hell; the third day He arose again from the dead; He ascended into Heaven, sitteth at the right hand of God, the Father Almighty; from thence He shall come to judge the living and the dead.

I believe in the Holy Ghost, the Holy Catholic Church, the communion of saints, the forgiveness of sins, the resurrection of the body, and life everlasting. Amen.

GOD made us and put us into this world to know Him and love Him, and to be happy with Him forever. He did not leave us to run around

like dogs and rabbits. Animals do not know why God made them. But we know why God made us. God Himself told us, and He made everything nice and plain.

He sent His own Son, Jesus, who taught us what we need to know. Jesus started His big Church that reaches all over the world, and will last till the end of the world. The church tells us just what Jesus said and what He meant, so we cannot go wrong.

Being good and getting to heaven are the most important things. We must not make any mistakes. God knows that, and He does not want us to worry.

The Apostles were the followers of Jesus, the first Bishops and priests of His Church. They gave us the Apostles' Creed. This long prayer tells us all the things we believe. How happy we are, to know so much about God!

There are still many people in the world who do not know these things. They do not know why they were born, nor where they may go when they die. They do not know that God loves them and takes care of them. How unhappy they are! Whenever we say the Apostles' Creed, we should say it for these people, too. We should ask God to send people to teach them so they can be happy, too.

The Apostles
Writing Down the Creed

An Act of Faith

O my God, I firmly believe that Thou art
One God in three Divine Persons,
Father, Son, and Holy Ghost;
I believe that Thy Divine Son became man,
and died for our sins, and that He
will come to judge the living
and the dead.
I believe these and all the truths which
the Holy Catholic Church teaches
because Thou hast revealed them,
who canst neither deceive nor
be deceived.

THE ACT OF FAITH is a short way of saying all that is in the Apostles' Creed. We ought to say it with love, thanking God for giving us the Catholic Faith. We ought to say it not only for ourselves, but for other people who do not believe in all the things God has taught us. Faith means believing what God teaches. God went to a great deal of trouble to teach us the things we ought to know about Him.

An Act of Hope

O my God, relying on Thy almighty power and infinite mercy and promises, I hope to obtain pardon of my sins, the help of Thy grace, and life everlasting, through the merits of Jesus Christ, my Lord and Redeemer.

T HE ACT OF HOPE means that we know God is good and kind. We know He loves us, and He takes care of us. We know Jesus died for us. God promised to keep us from all harm, and to take us to heaven forever, if we try to please Him. We know God keeps His promises. We can lie down and sleep every night in God's arms, and never worry a bit. People who worry very much are not trusting God as they should. We can ask God for everything we need, and be sure He will hear us.

80

An Act of Love

O my God, I love Thee above all things, with my whole heart and soul, because Thou art all-good and worthy of all love. I love my neighbor as myself for the love of Thee. I forgive all who have injured me, and ask pardon of all whom I have injured.

A N ACT OF LOVE means that we love God just because He is so nice and so good, so beautiful, so wonderful and wise. We love Him because He loves us, and always does such nice things for us. We also love other people, because God loves them. We forgive all the mean things others have done to us. And if we have done anything mean to anybody, we are sorry and will try to make up for it.

An Act of Contrition

O my God, I am heartily sorry for having offended Thee, and I detest all my sins, because of Thy just punishments, but most of all because they offend Thee, my God, who art all-good and deserving of all my love. I firmly resolve, with the help of Thy grace, to confess my sins, do penance and to amend my life, amen.

AN ACT OF CONTRITION means that we are sorry for all our sins. We are afraid, because we know God does not like anything bad or mean. Badness always has to be punished in some way. We are sorry most of all because we want to be God's good friends. God takes care of us all the time. If He stopped thinking about us and loving us even for a minute, we would turn into nothing! How can we do bad things, right before His eyes? Our sins made Jesus hurt, too, when He hung on the cross and died. We are sorry for our sins, and we make up our minds now, that we will never, never, never, do bad things again.

Prayer Before Meals

Bless us, O Lord, and these Thy gifts, which we are about to receive from Thy bounty, through Christ our Lord. Amen.

Dogs and cats, and pigs and horses run and begin eating as soon as they see their food. They are animals, not people. They do not know that God made everything. They cannot pray. But we are people. We do not run and begin to gobble up our food at once.

We stop a little, and remember that God made these things for us, and that He gives them to us. We ask God to bless us. That means to make us good and happy and holy, and to smile on us, His children. We ask God to bless our food, too. We ask God to do these things through Christ Our Lord. That means Jesus, our Lord, prays with us. We ought to think of many poor people and children who do not have much to eat. We should pray God to help them too.

Thanksgiving After Meals

We give Thee thanks for all Thy benefits, O Almighty God, who livest and reignest forever; and may the souls of the faithful departed, through the mercy of God, rest in peace. Amen.

WHEN we give somebody a present we think he has no manners if he takes it and goes away without saying thanks. After we have eaten God's gifts of good food, we should thank Him. We call Him Almighty God. That means God can do anything He wants to. He made this big world and all the things that grow on it, so we could have good food.

After we have thanked God for our food, we think of the many people who have died and who are not yet in heaven. They have to stay out until their souls are clean enough for heaven. We can help them by praying for them. It is nice to do this after every meal, so we will never forget.

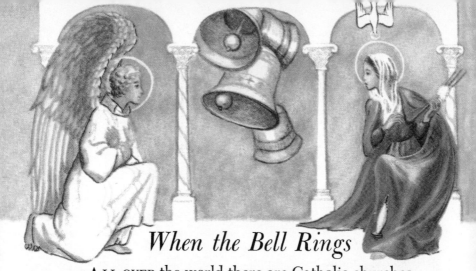

When the Bell Rings

ALL OVER the world there are Catholic churches, and nearly every church has a tall steeple with a bell in it. The church bell is a special thing. It rings to tell us to come to Mass, and it rings to tell us to pray for someone who has died. It also rings morning, noon, and night to tell us to say a special prayer called the Angelus.

This prayer reminds us of what the angel said to Mary, when God came down from heaven to be her little baby. It reminds us that God came to live with us, and die for us. That was the greatest thing that ever happened in the whole world. We never forget it. We ring the church bell three times every day, so we will think of this and thank God. We ask God's mother to pray for us specially at that time. This is the way we say the Angelus.

The Angelus

V. *The angel of the Lord declared unto Mary.*

R. *And she conceived of the Holy Ghost.*
(Then we say The Hail Mary prayer.)

V. *Behold the handmaid of the Lord.*

R. *Be it done unto me according to thy word.*

(Hail Mary, again)

V. *And the Word was made flesh.*

R. *And dwelt among us*

(Hail Mary, again)

V. *Pray for us, O holy Mother of God.*

R. *That we may be made worthy of the promises of Christ.*

Let us pray

Pour forth, we beseech Thee, O Lord, Thy grace into our hearts, that we to whom the Incarnation of Christ, Thy Son, was made known by the message of an angel, may by His passion and cross be brought to the glory of His resurrection, through the same Christ Our Lord. Amen.

Good Manners in Church

WHEN WE go into church we are going to visit in God's house. As soon as we come in the door we stop talking, laughing and looking around. We pay attention to Jesus. He is there waiting for us. He is in the Blessed Sacrament, on the altar. The little red lamp that burns day and night tells where He is.

We dip our fingers in the holy water and make the sign of the cross, carefully. We think of the Blood of Jesus, which washes away our sins.

Before we go in to our place, we bend our right knee down to the floor, to adore Jesus in the Blessed Sacrament. We do this if we pass from one side of the church to the other, and before we leave the church, too. As we do, we may say some small prayer, like, "Jesus, my God, I adore Thee."

When we are in our place we kneel down and talk to God. When we get tired kneeling, we can sit down. If we are at Mass or Benediction, there are prayers to say and maybe hymns to sing.

We can go into church at any time, when there is no service going on, just to visit Jesus. We may just have a little talk with Him, or we may wish to say a Rosary. We might kneel before the statue of Our Blessed Mother, or of Saint Joseph or some other saint, and say some prayers. But Jesus in the Blessed Sacrament must always come first.

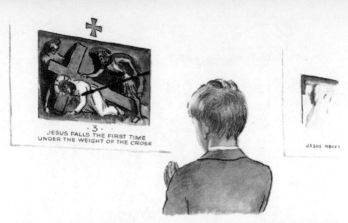

It is nice sometimes, especially on Fridays or in Lent, to make the Stations of the Way of the Cross. The fourteen pictures around the walls of the church show how Jesus carried His heavy cross and died for our sins. We can walk around and stand in front of each picture and think about it for a minute. We try to love Jesus, to make up for all the things bad people did to Him. At the end, we kneel before the altar and say some prayers for all those things the Holy Father in Rome is anxious about. These are, that everybody will know and love God, and that they will stop fighting wars, and be good.

It is nice to step into the church for a minute every time we pass by. If we are riding and cannot stop, we at least bow our heads (boys lift their hats) and say some little prayer, because Jesus is there in the church.

Hail, Holy Queen

Hail, Holy Queen, Mother of Mercy, hail our life, our sweetness, and our hope! To thee do we cry, poor banished children of Eve! To thee do we send up our sighs, mourning and weeping in this vale of tears. Turn then, most gracious advocate, thine eyes of mercy toward us; and after this, our exile, show unto us the blessed fruit of thy womb, Jesus! O clement, O loving, O sweet Virgin Mary!

MARY is God's mother. She took care of Jesus, the God-baby, when He was little. She made His clothes and cooked His meals and watched Him grow up and loved Him more than anybody in the world. When Jesus taught and helped people, Mary was often there close by, helping too. When Jesus died on the cross, Mary stood there beside Him, to show Him that she loved Him. Her heart was breaking, and she cried a lot that day. But she knew Jesus was dying to open heaven for us, and she loved us too. She was willing to give up her Son as a present to God for us.

After Jesus went back to heaven, Mary stayed in this world a long time, helping people. She told stories about Jesus when He was little, and a wise and holy man named Saint Luke wrote the stories in God's book. After a while, Jesus came and took His mother up to heaven. He made her the queen of heaven. All the people there love her as their mother. The great angels bow down to her. We pray to Mary for everything we want, especially to help us go to heaven. In the "Hail, Holy Queen" prayer we tell her that we are often sad and in trouble here, just as she was. We ask her to bring us to heaven when we die, and show us her son, Jesus.

The Confiteor

I confess to Almighty God, to blessed Mary ever Virgin, to blessed Michael the Archangel, to blessed John the Baptist, to the holy Apostles Peter and Paul, and to all the saints, that I have sinned exceedingly in thought, word, and deed, through my fault, through my fault, through my most grievous fault. Therefore, I beseech blessed Mary ever Virgin, blessed Michael the Archangel, blessed John the Baptist, the holy Apostles Peter and Paul, and all the saints, to pray to the Lord our God for me.

May the Almighty God have mercy on me, and forgive me my sins, and bring me to everlasting life. Amen.

May the Almighty and merciful Lord grant me pardon, absolution, and remission of all my sins. Amen.

THE "I Confess" prayer says that we are sorry for every bad thing we ever did. We know that God saw us do all those bad things. Mary, our Blessed Mother, and all the angels and saints in heaven saw us too. They were all sorry and ashamed to see us do those things. So we tell God and Blessed Mother about it. We tell Saint Michael, too. He is God's great soldier angel (the one who put the devil out of heaven). We tell all the saints too. We say it was all our fault, not anybody else's fault. We say we are terribly sorry, and we ask them all to pray to God for us. If they all pray hard, and we try hard, then we will be brave enough not to sin any more. We want to start all over, new and clean. We ask God to forgive us and help us and wash our souls all clean. We ask Him just to please forget all about the bad sins and put His arms around us and love us again. That is what the "I Confess" prayer means.

How to Go To Confession

Fɪʀsᴛ, we pray to the Holy Ghost to help us to do the five things needed for a good confession.

Come, Holy Ghost, Help Me

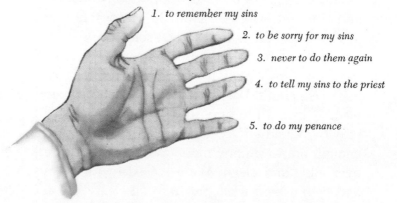

1. *to remember my sins*

2. *to be sorry for my sins*

3. *never to do them again*

4. *to tell my sins to the priest*

5. *to do my penance*

We try to remember all our sins. We think how good God is, and how He was looking at us all the time we were doing wrong. We tell Him we are sorry, and say the Act of Contrition. We say the "I Confess" prayer too, if we know it. We make up our minds never to do bad things again, and we promise God we won't.

Then we go into the confessional. We kneel down and make the Sign of the Cross. We say to the priest, "Bless me, Father. I have sinned." Then we tell him how long it is since we last went to confession, and say, "Since that time, I have . . ."

(Then we say our sins and how many times we did each one.)

We end our confession by saying: "I am sorry for these and all the sins of my past life, especially for. . . ." We tell some sin that we have confessed before, and that we are very sorry for.

We should listen to what the priest tells us. He will give us a penance to say. When he raises his hand and says the words that wash away our sins, we whisper the Act of Contrition. We think of Jesus sitting there in the priest's place, forgiving our sins and blessing us.

We go out then, and say our penance right away. We thank Jesus for forgiving our sins and making us all clean again. We promise Him to be good, and we ask Blessed Mother and our Angel to help us.

We pray for bad people so that they will be sorry and confess their sins and turn good. We pray for people who do not know that Jesus wants to forgive their sins.

Then we can go out and be very happy and jolly. Nobody in the world is so happy as a person whose sins are forgiven.

Being Friendly With God

WE HAVE learned some of the prayers that all Catholics must know. Prayers for Mass and Rosary are in other books. The prayers in this book are the shorter ones. These prayers are very wise and good. They show us how we ought to talk to God. The best one of these, of course, is the one God Himself taught us, the Our Father. It is a wonderful thing that we can talk to God, who is so great. We can talk to Him, and He listens! He even *wants* us to talk to Him. It makes Him glad and happy.

The way to talk to God is to talk with love. And one very good way is to use no special words at all, but just to be quiet and think about God. We can kneel or sit in church and think about God. Maybe we will say a few little words to Him, and then think some more. We know that we love Him, and He loves us, and that is enough. We can think about God when we are going about, or playing, or working. When we see a beautiful morning, we can think that God made it. We think how nice He is, and maybe we might say something like, "Dear God, it is an awfully nice morning. How did you ever make it so lovely?" We might see a kitten or a bird hopping. We might remember that God made these little things that are cute and pretty. We could just mention it to Him, to show Him that we notice and appreciate what He made. He likes to be appreciated.

Sometimes we might sit quietly in our room
for a little while, or lie in bed before we go to
sleep at night, and think about God.

 NEUMANN PRESS | *A collection of the finest*
Catholic children's books

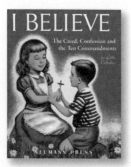

978-1-930873-35-3

978-0-911845-19-8

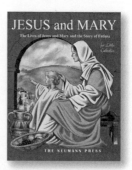

978-1-930873-42-1

978-0-911845-66-2

978-0-911845-67-9

978-0-911845-94-5

978-0-911845-95-2

978-0-911845-03-7

978-0-911845-04-4

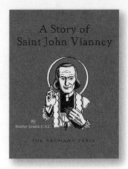

978-0-911845-30-3

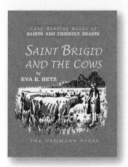

978-1-930873-95-7

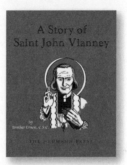

978-1-930873-96-4

978-1-930873-83-4

978-0-911845-46-4

978-0-911845-47-1

978-0-911845-48-8

978-0-911845-49-5

NEUMANN PRESS

Neumann Press, an imprint of TAN Books, publishes books and materials for children that educate, inspire, and assist their first steps in the Catholic faith.

Neumann Press was established in 1981 by the Dennis McCoy family. The Press became known and loved by thousands of customers for its nearly 200 classic Catholic titles, each one lovingly and expertly printed and bound by McCoy family members and friends.

In 2013 Neumann Press was acquired by TAN. Today Neumann Press continues to publish the vintage children and educational titles for which it is loved—as well as releasing new titles that raise the hearts and minds of children to God.

For a free catalog, visit us online at
NeumannPress.com

Or call us toll-free at
(800) 437-5876